WHAT PEOPLE ARE SAYING ABOUT

A QUIET MIND

This is a powerful book, because it is the fruit of lived experience. It is a necessary book because many people struggle with their minds in isolation, believing (as Eva did) that no one else feels the same. It is an important book because, with the authority of priesthood, Eva gives implicit permission for others to recount their stories and thereby be healed in the telling.

Simon Small
Author of *From the Bottom of the Pond*

Eva McIntyre uses her own journeying and the ways she has found helpful to encourage and support others who seek to live full, human, gifted and joyful lives. Her powers of evoking memory, place and emotion make this a powerful and life-giving book. I will certainly use it with people I journey with.

Revd Dr Chris Jenkins
Priest, Psychotherapist, Spiritual Director & Chair of the Association for Pastoral and Spiritual Care and Counselling

If you associate 'church' with lingering guilt or negative attitudes towards the body, this book will offer you the chance to explore for yourself the often forgotten but rich traditions of Christian spirituality which liberate and affirm. Eva McIntyre writes freshly and readably from the heart of her own experience.

Janet Morley
Author of *All Desires Known.*

Eva McIntyre is a very able and committed priest who longs to share the abundance of life that she has found through God's love in Jesus with others. In this book she shares her wisdom and her experience – painful as well as joyful – in a reflective, profound and often moving fashion. I commend it warmly to anyone who wants to find the wholeness that God yearns to give to everyone.

The Right Revd Dr John Inge,
Bishop of Worcester.

A Quiet Mind

Uniting Body, Mind and Emotions
in Christian Spirituality

A Quiet Mind

Uniting Body, Mind and Emotions
in Christian Spirituality

Eva McIntyre

BOOKS

Winchester, UK
Washington, USA

First published by O-Books, 2011
O-Books is an imprint of John Hunt Publishing Ltd., Laurel House, Station Approach,
Alresford, Hants, SO24 9JH, UK
office1@o-books.net
www.o-books.com

For distributor details and how to order please visit the 'Ordering' section on our website.

Text copyright: Eva McIntyre 2010

ISBN: 978 1 84694 507 6

A CIP catalogue record for this book is available from the British Library.

Design: Lee Nash

Printed in the UK by CPI Antony Rowe
Printed in the USA by Offset Paperback Mfrs, Inc

We operate a distinctive and ethical publishing philosophy in all
areas of our business, from our global network of authors to
production and worldwide distribution.

CONTENTS

Acknowledgements

I wish to thank John Hunt, Trevor Green and all at O Books for making this book possible.

Especial thanks to Simon Small for his kind and generous support, encouragement and advice.

My gratitude to the therapists who have worked with me over the years; Ellis, Chris, Susannah and Christine. Gratitude also to my theatre teachers David Vann, Mollie Guilfoyle and Andrew Potter and to my Tai Chi instructors Christine Swales and Raymond Towers.

And to all those friends and angels who have taught me by example throughout my life.

When the night seems long and heavy
I will shine the light of love to lead you through.
When you think you are all alone
I will send gentle angels to reassure you.
And when the cold of fear creeps into your heart
I will be a shield and a sword to protect you.
And in the morning, after the storm,
There will be peace and a quiet mind.

Foreword

One of my most abiding memories as a parish priest is a conversation with an elderly woman who had been attending church all her life. She could not accept that God loved her. She recoiled from the idea that she was a beautiful child of God, made in his image. Her mind was filled with disparaging thoughts about herself.

Although not the only cause, decades of negative teaching and self-abasing prayers had contributed to a deep sense of self-loathing. I have met a lot of such people, damaged by what the Church has taught about the nature of humanity.

Countless conversations with those who have left the Church confirm that this is a major issue. Very often such people have subsequently plunged into the innumerable alternative spiritualities that abound in the western world and found, to their delight, a wonderfully positive view of what it is to be a human being.

It is this question that Eva McIntyre addresses in "A Quiet Mind". Through reflecting on her personal journey, she offers thoughts, stories and gentle exercises that she has found helpful.

This is a powerful book, because it is the fruit of lived experience. It is a necessary book because so many people struggle with their minds in isolation, believing (as Eva did) that no one else feels the same. It is an important book because, with the authority of priesthood, Eva gives implicit permission for others to recount their stories and thereby be healed in the telling.

It is also a book from which the Church as an institution could learn much.

Simon Small
Author of "From the Bottom of the Pond: the forgotten art of experiencing God in the depths of the present moment".

I

A Quiet Mind

I used to think it was just me but now I know that it's not. I know because I asked other people and they said it happened to them, too.

For most of my life, I have experienced those critical, punishing thoughts in my head. The ones that tell me I'm useless, that I should do better, that my feelings are bad and inappropriate. Words that assure me that no-one could possibly love me because I'm ugly, unwanted and unlovable. The words in your head might be slightly different but they probably beat you up in a similar manner. You're too tall/short, too fat/thin, too stupid/geeky, too loud/quiet, too lazy/work orientated, too stubborn/a walkover etc. etc. etc. Please *don't* fill in the gaps!

The really nasty thing about these words isn't what they say but how they make me feel. Once I've managed to fill my head up with all the worst aspects of self-loathing, I feel really awful. When I feel awful, I start a whole new chain of horrible thoughts and then I feel even worse. If I keep it up for long enough, I can become depressed.

Once I'm in this negative place, I don't just stop there, oh no! I can follow it up with the most amazing plots and scenarios. I can run entire imaginary encounters full of negative outcomes to really put the cap on how badly I feel about myself! I can imagine conversations, arguments, betrayal and rejection, without even leaving my chair. I'm quite an expert at this. No-one had to teach me *how* to do it; it's simply the sum total of all the negative events and experiences of my life re-enacting themselves in a modern and entirely irrelevant context. It's a form of masochistic indulgence; punishing myself for a crime

3

that I can't remember because I never actually committed it!

What's even more sinister, is that this way of thinking is addictive. It's known and safe and in a really rather sick way, comfortable. It's much more scary to do something to change how I think and feel than it is to suffer this painful and degrading way of living.

However, misery isn't really a pleasant experience, even if we wallow as hard as we can! It never acquires for us those desires of our heart that underline these wretched words in our heads. Words that tell us we won't get what we want because we don't deserve it. Looking miserable won't draw positive people and opportunities towards us. What is more, changing these thought patterns isn't so painful or difficult and it leads to a brighter, fuller, happier life.

It is truly ironic that a way of life that claims to set us free, namely the teachings of Jesus, has for many turned into an emotional straightjacket. The Church's teaching has all too often reinforced low self-esteem and shame. In this book, I am exploring a different approach to Christian Spirituality; one that is holistic and brings together the mind, emotions and body in the quest to free the spirit and find wholeness. I will be looking at ways of overcoming negative patterns of thinking and feeling by using methods that I have learnt through my personal experience, my ministry as an Anglican priest and through the discoveries I have made on my own spiritual quest. This is a journey of healing, of moving towards a self-acceptance that includes the mind, emotions, body and spirit; the whole person. This is also a journey of daring to move closer to God and to find acceptance at the most profound level of our being. It is a journey of love and hope that gives us permission to take up our individual and unique journey of self-discovery and encounter; with others and with God.

I have drawn on the disciplines of psychology, theatre, prayer, tai chi and theology to arrive at this collection of techniques for working towards wholeness and healing; to achieve a quiet mind.

My first inspiration for this book came from a prayer written by Thomas Cranmer around 350 years ago for the 1662 Book of Common Prayer:

Grant, we beseech thee, merciful Lord, to thy faithful people pardon and peace; that they may be cleansed from all their sins, and serve thee with a quiet mind, through Jesus Christ our Lord. Amen.

A Cherokee story

A Grandson came to his old Grandfather and told him how he was very angry with a friend who had done him an injustice. The Grandfather said, "I have struggled with these feelings many times. It is as if there are two wolves inside me; one is good and does no harm. He lives in harmony with all around him. The other wolf, ah! The littlest thing will send him into a frenzy. He fights everyone, all the time, for no reason. He cannot think because his anger and hatred are so great. Sometimes it is hard to live with these two wolves inside me, for both of them try to dominate my spirit."

The boy looked intently into his Grandfather's eyes and asked, "Which one wins, Grandfather?"

The Grandfather smiled and said quietly, "The one I feed."

Learning to change the words in our heads is the first lesson in learning to love and respect ourselves. When I think about the negative thoughts I have about myself, I know I would never speak to another human being in this appalling manner, so why on earth do I think it's acceptable to talk to myself in this way?!

The first step in changing the pattern is to recognise that it is bad; or to use another, often misused word and to do so correctly, it is *sinful*. I don't use this word lightly; sin is whatever brings imbalance into our lives and damages relationships; negative thought patterns are at the beginning of all imbalance: fix them and you fix the beginnings of sin.

The Church needs to recognise the role it has played in perpetuating these negative patterns of thought and behaviour. Somewhere along the road, being perfect became about being right and never making mistakes, rather than about being complete. Our relationship with a loving Creator who yearns to meet us, was turned into a system of rules and regulations, mostly involving grovelling and feeling unworthy before a divinity that demands we do the impossible.

When I was a child, my mother told me that God (an old man in the sky) had a book and in that book, the name of every human being on earth was written. Every time we do something wrong, God puts a black mark by our names. The inference being that, when you pop your clogs, God tots up the black marks to see where you will spend eternity. I was a child, I was too wise to believe this rubbish but I assumed my mother believed it, so I humoured her. It was only later that I saw it was simply one way she used to attempt to control my behaviour. I look at many of the practices of the Church over the centuries and indeed today and see the same thing.

Professor Gareth Lloyd Jones said in a sermon a few years ago, "The Hebrews repented not by feeling bad but by thinking differently." If we change our thoughts, we change our feelings and our behaviour. If we change our behaviour, we change our lives and our world.

The clues that lead to a different reading and practice of Christianity are all in the New Testament; not just different interpretations of the same texts that have so often been used to make people smaller, more controllable but also texts that are skimmed over and whose true value is unrealised through overfamiliarity. Jesus had a great ability to make people feel worthy, loveable, accepted even, or perhaps especially, people who felt rejected and condemned by society and the religious leaders of their time. The

Samaritan woman at the well with her many husbands and live-in lover, Zacchaeus the corrupt tax collector, the slave of a Roman Centurion, a woman of 'ill repute' with a bottle of perfume. All of these people were not only inspired by Jesus but recognised their own worth through an encounter with him. If we are to take our own spiritual journey towards wholeness seriously, we too must take up the challenge of understanding our relationship with God and its implications for our own worthiness in the light of Jesus' relationships, as well as his teaching.

So how do we begin this process of changing our negative thought patterns? One thing is sure; we won't succeed if we beat ourselves up about the negative thoughts!

I have found trying to push them away pretty futile, too; it tends to turn into an argument between different parts of me inside my head.

There are four ways that I *have* found helpful:

Firstly, to 'give them up'; for Lent or another appropriate period of time. This may sound daft but it has worked as a period of getting used to not indulging in the practice. Each time I catch myself descending into a negative thought pattern, I say to myself, 'that's a negative thought pattern and I've given those up!' Naming them, seems to give me some power over them; I recognise them as something separate and under my control. As soon as I shine the spotlight of reality upon them, they cease their chattering and are powerless to hurt me. This works particularly well with the long and involved negative stories that I can create for myself.

Secondly, listen to them and accept them before disagreeing with and dismissing them. I say 'thank you for your opinion' to whichever part of me is being critical and it seems to work; that part of me feels acknowledged and I know the internal discussion is over.

Thirdly, when you think something negative about yourself, ask the question 'Who taught me that?' Tracing the negative thought back to its origins, be it something you were told as a child or something you learnt through a painful experience at some stage in your life, helps to show that the thoughts belong in the past and not the present. By realising where the negative lessons were learnt, we can begin the process of placing them back where they belong, instead of carrying them around with us, like a rucksack.

Fourthly, practising positive thought patterns. This is the antidote to the negative variety! Take time each day to tell yourself some positive things. Praise yourself for things you have done well. Acknowledge your good qualities and assets. If you have low self-esteem about your appearance, focus on something about yourself that you like and about which other people compliment you, then praise and savour it; 'I have lovely eyes' or 'My skin is clear and soft' etc. Likewise for other areas of life; if you have spent years believing yourself to be stupid, focus on something you have achieved and acknowledge the qualities you needed to do that thing.

I would advise starting with the small things, until you get used to receiving your own praise. If you have spent a lifetime feeling like something that you would scrape off the bottom of a shoe, it will feel very strange to be hearing and acknowledging good things about yourself. So start with the little things: small acts, qualities, areas of achievement, until you learn how to handle the praise. Sit with the discomfort the praise creates and feel it; try not to slip into the pattern of denying the good thing about yourself in order to rid yourself of the discomfort. If you do slip up, acknowledge that this is what you have done and why you have done it, then repeat the good thing to yourself. Say it out loud if you really can't drown the negativity with your internal voice.

When you've been practising for a while, notice how your mood is affected by these positive thoughts. Just as the negative thoughts bring you down, so the positive ones will lift you. When you can handle the positive thoughts about the small things, move on to the larger things in your life and work at those, too. Don't worry if you slip back and forget, you can always begin again at any moment.

The final part of the process is to have these positive thoughts at hand for when the negative ones strike! When that old voice thunders in with a criticism, you can counter it with something positive: get in before it makes you feel bad and replace it with words that will make you feel good about yourself.

Use this practice with memories, too; so often it's the negative memories we recall, the painful, difficult times and not the happy ones. This is probably because of the way in which negative experiences, 'failures', disappointments, shape us. They are critical in building up our coping and survival techniques. However, the positive, happy memories are the ones that feed our natural disposition and we do well to call on them to feed the sunny side of our nature.

We are all a work in progress; you are worth the effort of that work. Even in the midst of difficult circumstances, we have a choice as to whether we view our cup as half full or half empty. We can choose to be either miserable or happy as a general approach to life. It might feel like a struggle to break down years of habit but the gain is worth the struggle and the power to make the change lies within each one of us.

One of the most moving memories that I have from my time as a prison chaplain, is that of the confirmation of two women in the little prison chapel. Both of the women had survived horrendous childhood experiences and gone on to live lives dominated by drug addiction, which they paid for through crime and prostitution. Their journeys in faith were remarkable ones and the day of the confirmation was charged with a variety of emotions for us all. When the moment came for them to kneel before the bishop to be confirmed, the whole enormity of the occasion overwhelmed them. The bishop was wearing sandals and I watched as the women's tears splashed onto his feet and suddenly the story of the woman in Luke's gospel, weeping over the feet of Jesus, became utterly real to me! These women had brought their brokenness and belief of their utter worthlessness and found acceptance and healing. They knew themselves to be loved not only by the people around them but by God.

2

Stilling the Monkey Mind

"Whatever is true, whatever is noble, whatever is right, whatever is pure, whatever is lovely, whatever is admirable, if anything is excellent or praiseworthy, think about such things." Philippians 4: 8

One of the common difficulties expressed by those who meditate and contemplate, is the issue of stilling the chattering mind or the 'monkey mind' as Eastern tradition refers to it. As soon as the body is still, we notice how active the conscious mind is; racing around, leaping from one thought to another; clutching at worries and anxieties, desperately doing anything but cease its incessant chattering. A moment of stillness is sometimes found, until we recognise it and another few thoughts pop in to fill the space.

In the Christian tradition, there is a difference between Meditation and Contemplation; the difference is in Words. Meditation will use a phrase, a story, a mantra, a thought or an image (an icon or a picture) to begin its journey. It uses this as something to ponder, to turn over in the mind as you draw close to the Divine in time, present time. Contemplation moves away from words, thoughts, or thoughts held within images, towards stillness and an emptiness that is utterly full of energy, of the Divine. In stillness and waiting, contemplation brings us into the present moment to meet God.

Meditation is what happens when we ponder in the presence of the Divine. We take a saying, reading, phrase, image, problem and we roll it around with God and await whatever results in our feelings and thoughts. It is so easy to forget that our Creator is intimately interested in our lives and that, unlike all our human confidantes, can see all sides of the picture and holds time in a completely different focus. Meditation can happen anywhere at anytime but you may find you have favourite places that help you and certain times are easier. I knew a young mum who would feign constipation because her only chance for quiet meditation was to lock herself in the bathroom. She did what she had to do. Our spiritual well-being is an essential component in our total health and is neglected at our peril.

There are countless practices we can do to try to still the mind during meditation and contemplation but they will all be hampered if we do not address the obvious fact; that, we cannot expect our minds to suddenly cease their frenetic activity and change gear in a moment or even in an hour. The more we try, the more tension we will introduce and the more stimulated the mind will become. The place to start, is not in the meditation space but the time and space surrounding it. We need first to calm and slow the mind in the rest of our lives; to un-clutter it before we can expect it to cease its chattering when we meditate. The process of letting go of the ceaseless tide needs to begin in our daily lives; in our work and recreation activities in order to bring a less chattering mind into meditation.

In this way, we take away the distinction between the meditative or spiritual and the rest of life. We stop seeing these moments of stillness as a pause in our day or week, when we charge up our spiritual battery and then toddle back into the mania and mayhem of the 'real world'. All life becomes spiritual and within it are times of great activity and times of real stillness but they are connected, they are different parts of the same story that is our lives. The stillness is the anchor, the grounding of our existence; our actions move from that firm place; our voices speak from that place of security. We are still and firm at the core of our being, balanced so that we may rock or falter but never be permanently knocked to the floor. Rather like those children's toys from the 1970s, 'Weebles wobble but they don't fall down'.

We can only find this stable centre within ourselves if we treat our lives as one whole; not a series of compartments into which we enter and exit. It has been a tendency with so many people to divide up their lives, as though some bits are 'holy' and others are not; some bits worthy of our attention and some not. Worse, still, some bits acceptable to God and some not. Yet, if our spirituality is to be relevant to us, it must encompass the whole of our lives, flowing seamlessly from one moment to the next. The God Jesus spoke about is as intimately interested in our working and playing as in our praying. Jesus was vocal about what was most important to God, perhaps most famously in those words "The Sabbath was made for man, not man for the Sabbath" (Mark 2:27) The story of the wedding at Cana in John's gospel tells of a man who knew how to have fun and celebrate and considered these things as equally worthy of his attention as teaching about God and healing the sick .The early Christian Celts certainly saw no distinction between sacred and secular, worship and work; their whole lives flowed without boundaries from one task to another. There was nothing that could not be the subject of prayer; dressing, sleeping, milking the cow, lighting the fire: all were seen as being as worthy of prayer as those acts we would call religious and restrict to Church services. There was no area of their lives that they did not believe God to be passionately and intimately involved in. Their model of faith, life and community can offer a great deal to our often polarised and divided existences in the modern world. It is no accident that Celtic Spirituality has become such a popular topic in our fragmented world. If we create boundaries in our lives, those boundaries will fight within our minds when we come to stillness and prayer. In prayer, we need to be boundary-less, open; bring our all as one complete being into the oneness of creation and creator.

This does not mean we take down our boundaries or coping mechanisms in relation to other people; rather, the spiritual life can lead us into a greater, healthier understanding of appropriate boundaries between ourselves and other people and those between us and the society in which we live. The boundaries we need to address to stop the monkey mind, are the ones within ourselves. All we need, is to be aware of these boundaries; that they sit within us but they do not define us. I may take a different stance and perspective into the workplace from the one I adopt at home but these two stances are not separate; there are not two (or more) of me; Me is at the core and centre and the stances I take in different environments and situations are actions I take but they do not define me. They are expressions, they are momentary not eternal. At the core of my being is my eternal identity; that which is inextricably linked to the eternal identity of the Divine, of all other people and of the whole of creation.

If we clutter up our lives with ceaseless thinking and frenetic activity, we cannot feel the core of our being or hear its voice; for to hear it, we need to be still and quiet, anchored; we need to be focussed.

Focus is the key to stilling the monkey mind both in our many daily activities and in those times we set aside for meditation and contemplation; the times of stillness between activities. When we are absorbed in an activity, it takes us over; we are not plagued with chattering thoughts, it is difficult to distract us. We are truly focussed on our activity and often, this will lead to a physical stillness where we only make those movements we need to make for the activity. We will only think the thoughts we need to think and say the words we need to say. The mind's butterfly eye turns into the cat's eye; steady and absorbed, beyond distraction unless a larger call for our attention is made.

When we focus, we are in the present moment; here and now: not heading back to the past or racing off into the future. In the meditative, spiritual lifestyle we seek to live always in the present moment. This moment is all we have; the past and future do not exist and we can effect no change upon them. In *this* moment is life and possibility. It is that sense of 'now-ness' that we need to bring to all our activities, if we are to still the monkey mind in the active and still areas of our lives.

Even in our moments of escapism, we can apply ourselves fully to the experience of visualising what we desire; to our daydreaming. When life is hard and we are surrounded by the negative energy of other people, we can detach from them and be truly ourselves in this present moment, whether by applying ourselves to the task in hand or by escaping into the creative realms of our minds. What we do, we do fully, now.

It's not complicated but it is not easy because it necessitates grappling with the restless tendencies of the conscious mind. It asks you, in all your activities, to constantly bring your attention, your focus, to this moment with its smells, sounds, sights and sensations; to the person you are talking with, the activity in which you are engaged. Each time you are drawn away into the past and future, acknowledge it and return to the present moment. Distinguish when a thought is in the present moment but dealing with a future activity (e.g. planning an event) and when it is in the realm of future fantasy (worrying about what might go wrong with the event). Root yourself in the present moment and make it the place from which all your words and actions spring. A strong centre, a still place, a state your conscious mind recognises. A practice which becomes natural and begins to be your predominate state of mind.

When we tackle the monkey mind in all our daily existence, it will hamper us less in our meditation and contemplative prayer.

Exercise

To bring yourself into the present moment, try the following practice and adapt it to suit your needs. (After you have tried it while reading the text, put down the book and go through the exercise alone.)

In whatever posture you find yourself (if you have the opportunity to find a comfortable posture, do) bring your attention to the front of your face; the central panel that encompasses your brow, eyes, nose, mouth and chin.

Next, focus your eyes on something; look at it but do not allow yourself to describe it in your head.

Keeping your eyes focussed on the object, take in the sounds that reach you and listen to them, again without putting words to them.

Now be aware of what you feel; a breeze or the warmth from a heater, the hardness or softness of a chair etc.

Notice how still your mind has become, how your heart is at ease in its rhythm, your breathing has become un-laboured and the energy in your body is placed low into the abdomen and pelvis. Now you are grounded and centred in this moment.

Prayer for stillness

God of tranquillity take my anxiety and quiet my soul
God of serenity take my busy-ness and still my mind
God of peace take my fears and calm my heart. Amen.

3

A Peaceful Heart

"Do not let your hearts be troubled. Trust in God, trust also in me." John 14: 1

Feelings are, of course, a natural and essential part of our lives. When they are healthy, they lead us to act and respond to others and the world around us in an appropriate and productive manner. When they are unhealthy or out of control, they can lead to destruction for ourselves and those around us. The feelings between a mother and her child are a useful benchmark as we look at feelings.

I remember a doctor once telling me about her experiences of delivering babies. She said that, at the moment of birth you have insight into the future each child is promised. She illustrated this with the stories of two babies she had delivered. The first was about a mother who, when her baby was being carried to her arms, called out, 'It's mine! It's mine!' The second told of a mother who, when handed her baby, looked into her face and said, 'Ooh! Hello!'

Mothers have a heavy load to carry in the expectations, pressure and responsibility placed upon them as they try, mostly untrained, to do their best at mothering their children from the resources of their human abilities. They can be a parable for all of us; for the way in which we nurture ourselves, those we love and the world in which we live. Each of us is limited by our own capabilities. Too often we are limited by the emotional handicaps that have been passed down to us, sometimes through many generations, by our families via our early life experiences. "The sins of the fathers are visited upon the sons"; not a threat but a statement of fact. The good news, however, is that we can break the chain; we do not have to repeat the patterns.

Of course, we have to start from where we are, we can't wipe the slate clean and pretend the past never happened and it hasn't left its imprint upon us. However, where we are is the best place to start and if we have kept our promise of not beating ourselves up, we will be able to assure ourselves that the shape we're in is not too bad at all and there are only some adjustments of confidence and habit to deal with.

When things go wrong with feelings, they can take us to one of two extremes. We can become overwhelmed by our feelings and therefore avoid situations that trigger them or we can put them into deep freeze and be unaware of them. Neither is healthy but they are normal reactions to an emotional imbalance in threatening circumstances. When we are young, we learn our own ways of coping with difficult, frightening or distressing things over which we have no control. Children have to learn these coping mechanisms because they are powerless in an adult world. Sometimes these coping mechanisms are peculiar, unhelpful for relationships or life limiting but they are the coping mechanisms we have learnt and should not be tampered with unless or until we have learnt new ways of coping. In a physical equivalent to this emotional situation; no-one would suggest that while hanging by your fingertips from a cliff face you should let go until you have something else to hold on to!

I remember hearing a therapist say the words, 'But they're only feelings!' to me and internally shrinking and wondering how she could say 'only' about something so vast and overwhelming. Now I understand that she wasn't belittling my feelings but encouraging me to see them in perspective and take control, rather than allowing them to rule my life. Love, fear, anger, frustration, sorrow; all feelings have a wonderful role to play in our experience of life and inspiring us to compassion for each other; they should never be our jailors.

When we do not deal justly with our feelings, they fester inside us until we cannot contain them any longer and they rise like projectile vomit, covering anyone in range. The mess we have to clear up is far more substantial than after a child's stomach bug, however. I often come across people who seem to be carrying pools of petrol around inside them that will erupt into a blazing inferno at the least provocation, as though a lit match has been tossed in their direction. The reaction far outweighs the issue because it is the sum total of the unspent feelings about events and injustices dating back many years, sometimes a whole lifetime. It is a tragedy that people suffer in this way when there is no need! It is unfair that others should be splattered by their feelings and relationships damaged through something that does not even relate to the present reality. The festering feelings can be exorcised, the dangerous petrol inside can be siphoned off without harm to others.

Apart from damaging our relationships with those around us, if we do not deal with unhealthy emotions, they will damage our relationship with God. After all, if we feel worthless, dirty, ashamed, guilty or resentful, we are hardly going to feel comfortable in the presence of the all-loving, perfect Divine, are we?! So we will avoid God and the healing and strengthening presence of divine energy and love. We will spurn and reject God because of our own preoccupation with our feelings. If negative thought patterns are the roots of sin, negative feelings are the shoots that grow from those roots.

I have met many people both within the Church and outside it, who have been unable to accept that they could possibly be loved by God; that they are worthy of such love. This doubt always stems from their own sense of unworthiness which they often learnt from the words and behaviour of others during their childhood. One memory particularly stands out; that of a woman in her forties, a good, conscientious, Christian woman who had no remarkable sins or crimes to recall; a loving mother and a kind friend. She broke down in despair after an evening service and when I asked her the cause of her distress, she explained that it had been the Psalm we had read. The words of the psalm had described how God's love and forgiveness would be extended to everyone. 'But I know that doesn't include me!' she explained. She could not logically account for why she should be excluded but her conviction was absolute; she felt unworthy of God's love. It was no good just telling her that she was wrong or trying to use words to convince her that the reality was quite different from her perception. This was a journey she needed to take in discovering the origins of her feelings before letting go of the wrongly learnt lessons.

Some of the most impressive lessons in love that I have experienced, have come from unexpected encounters. A while ago, a friend visited my house for the first time and being an animal lover, he was keen to make friends with my cat and to make her feel as unthreatened by his presence as possible. We were chatting in the kitchen while I prepared a meal and I was a bit perplexed to see him get up from his chair and lie on the floor. I was being very 'British' and so I didn't say 'What on earth are you doing down there?!' My cat, who had appeared in the doorway, seemed to be wondering the same thing, she turned tail and ran. My friend was disappointed by this, "Oh! I was trying to get lower than her, so she wouldn't be frightened and she might come to me!" he explained.

Some months later, I was discussing the way in which Jesus tried to express God's love to the people around him with some parishioners and this story popped into my mind, so I shared it with them. All of a sudden, I realised that it was a wonderful parallel to the story of the incarnation! Just like my friend, lying on the kitchen floor to get lower than my cat, so we can see in the story of Jesus, God's endeavour to get small enough and low enough in order that we won't be frightened and might come close. That is surely the message behind Luke's inclusion of shepherds looking into a manger at the baby Jesus; God made small, vulnerable and low in order for us to dare to believe that we are significant, loved, precious.

We are continually offered opportunities, challenges to come close, to believe in that love and to follow as is so beautifully expressed in the words of the song 'The Summons' by John Bell and Graham Maule,

Will you come and follow me if I but call your name?
Will you go where you don't know and never be the same?
Will you let my love be shown
Will you let my name be known
Will you let my life be grown
In you, and you in me?

To learn new ways of experiencing and dealing with our feelings, we have to practice. We have to unlearn our old ways and learn fresh ones. The first step is acknowledging the feelings; if we deny or suppress them, they will rise up to haunt us. The second step is to learn to let go of them; to not allow them to overwhelm you. Naming a feeling gives us power over it; when I feel a wave of loneliness overtake me, I stop and say 'I recognise that; it's loneliness; I've felt it before and it didn't kill me.' I allow myself to experience the loneliness, even if it makes me cry, remembering that, however bad it feels, I am in control, not the feeling of loneliness. Then I announce 'time up' and tell myself that I'm going to let go of the loneliness now because I have other feelings to draw upon and use to my benefit for whatever task I have to do.

As with our negative thoughts, our negative feelings are often rooted in having learnt the wrong lessons in childhood. We have got into a habit of feeling about ourselves in a particular way. It could be that someone intentionally taught us to feel badly about ourselves or we may have learnt something that wasn't intended.

For example; as we were growing up, adults were always saying how pretty my older sister was and how intelligent I was. They thought they were paying us compliments but the wires got crossed, resulting in her 'learning' that she was stupid and me 'learning' that I was ugly!

Children learn all sorts of 'hidden' lessons; parents who are overzealous to encourage the best school results can teach a child that his/her best is never good enough. A home environment where a child's emotional needs are not readily met can 'teach' that his/her feelings are inappropriate or worthless. Often, it takes years for us to even realise that we have learnt these lessons about ourselves. However, once we realise where the feelings have their origins; when we place the wrongly learnt lessons back in their original context, it becomes quite a simple process to disentangle them from our everyday lives and to teach ourselves new truths about ourselves which lead to more positive feelings.

It is quite remarkable to notice how differently people respond to us when we have more self-respect, when we love and appreciate ourselves. This is for a number of reasons; we set our boundaries differently when we respect ourselves; we are clearer about what is acceptable and what is not when it comes to how we are treated. We give clearer signals about our feelings on subjects or towards people because we have the confidence to know that how we feel is acceptable and should be respected. We will smile more because we are happier and people are much keener to be around happy people than miserable, angry or anxious ones!

Finally, when we have understood and nurtured our own inner world, we will be aware that everyone else is carrying around an inner world and we will be more sensitive and compassionate. Once we are freed from the debilitation of our own fear of feeling, we will be free to put down our self-absorption and truly care about others and we will be able to face our loving creator, confident that we will not be rejected.

Exercise

Sit or stand in front of the mirror and pay yourself a compliment. It is best to say it out loud. When you have heard the compliment, notice how you feel; where in your body do you feel a physical reaction to the compliment? What is the sensation? How do you feel about the sensation? If it is uncomfortable, acknowledge it. Explore the physical sensation and the feeling that goes with it. What is the emotion you are feeling? Why, do you think, are you experiencing that emotion? Stay with the emotion and really feel it. When you are ready, step back from the emotion and let it go for now.

Next, close your eyes and place your hand over your heart. Breathe deeply and slowly three times; in through your nose and out through your mouth. Call to mind a really happy experience in your life. Enjoy the moment again, in your mind. What physical sensations do you notice? What feeling accompanies them? Stay with that feeling and let it envelope you. When you are ready, remove your hand from your heart, breathe deeply 3 times again and open your eyes.

Prayer of invocation

I draw down the peace of God
I draw up the power of God
I draw in the love of God.

4

The Demon Fear

"Fear not, for I have redeemed you; I have called you by name; you are mine" Isaiah 43:1

The most overwhelming of our emotions and the most debilitating, is the natural state of fear. In an environment where most of us are not continually threatened by predators and danger, the absence of sufficient food or shelter, it would be reasonable to expect fear to be an uncommon experience. Yet fear is everywhere; it is the driving force of the lives of so many people in our modern, Western world. It manifests itself in so many ways: fear that we will not be good enough, that we will not fit in, that we will not be successful, that our dreams will turn to dust. All of these really hide one great fear; the fear of rejection. We are pack animals and like all pack animals, we have a deep and burning need to belong. Our identity is shaped by our place in the pack and conformity = survival.

With the nature and existence of the pack so vastly changed by our modern society, we have become confused about our identity and place. We have lost the security of knowing our place and role and are plagued by insecurity. This opens the door for fear to latch on to our every day existence and the easiest of place is within our own thought patterns. We conjure up scenarios to be feared, we transfer early fears into our present reality, we view others as having power over us, the ability to destroy us in some way. The result is immobility; we are frozen by our fears and stop being the shapers of our own destiny; we stagnate; we exist, rather than truly live.

One common response to fear is to seek to control life; to

control our environment, other people, events, the world around us. At its most extreme, this turns people inwards and results in obsession and attendant rituals, suspicion, hostility and ultimately, the very loneliness that drove the fear in the first place. In truth, we do not achieve mastery over our fear either by stupefying inactivity or by overpowering control. In both of these responses, we remain prisoners. The true antidotes to fear are trust and hope. The best approach to the emotion itself, is to recognise it for what it is; an emotion. To bring it down to its appropriate size and deal with the circumstances in which it arose, taking away its foundation.

Fear can also become a habit, and then an excuse for not making changes, for not achieving our potential, for not living our lives. All negative emotions thrive in situations of comfortable but comfortless mediocrity. We all, to varying degrees, fear the same things; intimacy, love, our own potency, success, acceptance. It is ironic that the very things we most crave, should also make us most afraid! We mistake cautiousness for safety and risk taking for danger. Yet the truth is, if we never take a risk, we never really live. The fear of something is so often far worse an experience than the event itself. The Christian call is to face the fear and dare to believe in love, dare to believe that you are capable of co-operating with God, as verse four of John Bell and Graham Maule's 'The Summons' illustrates:

Will you love the 'you' you hide
If I but call your name?
Will you quell the fear inside,
And never be the same?
Will you use the faith you've found
To reshape the world around
Through my sight and touch and sound
In you, and you in me?

Fear, unless we are in immediate danger (when it is of use to motivate us to self-preservation), belongs to either the past or the future. This is why hope is an effective antidote, for hope belongs only to the present moment. It's important to make a clear distinction between hope and wishing here. Wishing is an activity that has inbuilt disappointment value. It involves part of us rushing off into the future in search of something we do not yet possess and it results in us missing present opportunities. We tend to wish for things that are at some level unattainable; things we do not feel we can bring about ourselves. As we throw the penny into the wishing well, we toss both our dreams and our fears of them not coming to fruition with it. Wishes and disappointment are twins that will never be separated. Hope, on the other hand, involves an active waiting that knows that something is happening right now. Hope anchors us in the present moment. Hope gives us a sense of perspective and of power.

If I am fully present to this moment now, I can *do* something, I can *change* things, piece by tiny piece, second by second. Given that most other people will not be living in this present moment, I am suddenly aware of my inherent power to make this moment what I will it to be, while they are busy in the past and future, over which they have no real control.

Trust, too, is a tool to conquer fear. Trust brings us allies and sends the loneliness of fear away. Trust is not blind and must be won; we know from our past experiences the signals of those who can be trusted and those who cannot and we need to rely on those instincts. Trust is a two-edged sword because there is a sense in which it is unfair to trust someone else utterly for that turns the trust from being a garland of honour, to a yoke of slavery. We must be gentle and realistic in our trust, never mistaking it for an excuse to abdicate the responsibility for our emotional, mental, spiritual or physical safety. That said, the rewards that the trust of loved ones brings to us include the forgetting of fear and the appreciation of the present moment and therefore aids hope. Fear lives and breeds best in isolation.

When I was a child, my cousin and I would go to the local swimming pool. Neither of us were 'water babies'. We were afraid to jump in off the side and so my mother recruited the assistance of an older girl who held our hands and jumped in with us. We happily jumped, our fear gone. Unbeknown to us, my mother had paid her sixpence to let go of our hands on the third jump! Nothing awful happened, we lived to tell the tale and the fear had been taken out of the experience of jumping in, albeit at the shallow end. The shallow end, is of course, the best place to start.

The ancient Celtic Christians knew fear well; they lived in an uncertain world and felt the imminence of danger and loss acutely. One spoilt harvest could make the difference between life and death. Life's fragility was all around them and their faith was shaped by their experiences. They wove their faith into their lives to protect them from the uncertainty of the world around them as we can see in the words of St Patrick's breastplate;

I bind unto myself today
The strong arm of the Trinity
By invocation of the same
The Three in One and One in Three.

Although our lives are very different from our Celtic ancestors, our fears are as real and our faith can be woven into our lives to give us the same comfort and assurance. Reminding ourselves by such words as those of St Patrick can help to stem anxiety and the sense of powerlessness that accompanies it. Having the words to memory is an old practice that works for us in our modern world, too.

Christ be with me, Christ within me,
Christ behind me, Christ before me,
Christ beside me, Christ to win me
Christ to comfort and restore me.
Christ beneath me, Christ above me,
Christ in quiet, Christ in danger,
Christ in hearts of all that love me,
Christ in mouth of friend and stranger.

In the practice of casting out fear, meditation and contemplation are the most powerful of all tools. Jesus said, 'Perfect love casts out fear'. Just like that! Lucky Jesus, eh? Well, not quite. The same Jesus cried from the cross in terrible agony, 'My God, My God, why have you forsaken me?' We can tell ourselves he was quoting Psalm 22 and so it doesn't really count; he didn't really feel the fear of abandonment. However, the guy was hanging on a cross and gasping for breath, so why would he waste it on singing a hymn? Of course he felt abandoned, whether he actually uttered this Psalm word for word or not. The point is, he knew what he was talking about; he knew fear and he knew love. He knew divine love and whether he could feel it or not, it was always there, constantly poured out like the water from the mountains. And divine love is constantly there for each of us, too. It is in the air we breathe, the light that shines from the sun on the brightest or dullest day, the water of the seas and rivers, the green of nature, the breath of all living creatures, the heartbeat of creation echoed in our own chests. Meditation and contemplation bring us into immediate contact with that divine love, the energy of God.

A conversation I had, some years ago, with a man after the death of his mother profoundly concerned me. He described his prayer life to me; every night he would kneel beside his bed and say his prayers. These prayers, he explained, fell into two categories: people who were alive and people who had died.

'Now', he said, 'Mum has to move from the list of people who are alive to the list of those who have died alongside Dad'. Here was a man in his thirties whose prayer life had not moved on from the days of his childhood. How on earth was this going to help him through the loss of his mother, so close in time to the loss of his father? I wondered how many other members of my congregations were struggling along with equally unsatisfying prayer habits. It led me to develop a whole series of sermons on prayer.

Later, when I became a prison chaplain, I became concerned at the frequency with which women would ask me to pray for them and their families because they didn't really believe God would listen to them. I, on the other hand, must have a hotline and be a better person because I was ordained! I realised that persuading them that God was absolutely interested in their prayers was going to be a long term challenge.

When I talk to godparents before baptising children, I point out that one of the most important jobs of a godparent is to pray for the child. Frequently, I see terror growing in their eyes and it is quite clear that they think they don't have a clue how to pray and probably share the notion of my women prisoners, that God wouldn't want to listen to them, anyway. Yet prayer is actually such a natural thing and so accessible. I have found that children as young as four years old take to Contemplative prayer like ducks to water! I simply say to them 'Let's sit very quietly; check what you can hear; be aware of your heart beating, feel the air around you; see if you can feel God close'. It's amazing to watch them sink effortlessly into stillness and peace! It's usually the adults present who begin to fidget and struggle.

I have heard many talks about how to contemplate. I have tried most of the ideas I've heard or found in books. What I have discovered is that *trying* doesn't work for me. *Trying* ties me up in my own attempts and over stimulates my conscious mind, throwing me into a turmoil of thoughts that I vainly attempt to push out, accommodate or let go tied to balloons, depending upon which technique I'm following. As a student at theological college and subsequently as a curate, I set aside half an hour each day at the same time to contemplate at the suggestion of my spiritual director. I spent most of those half hours noticing how uncomfortable I was and battling unsuccessfully with the wandering of my mind. Just occasionally, I would glimpse a moment of stillness with God, only to lose it as soon as I recognised it.

I now realise that the Divine lives in moments, not half hours. To regulate God in such a way is to operate a divine appointment system! God is present now; in this moment and that is where to experience Divine encounter. I have abandoned techniques and methods; I have given up set prayer times and the reward has been to meet the divine at every and any moment and sometimes, I'm aware of it. Always when I bring myself to be fully present in the moment, I *feel* Divine presence and it is beautiful and joyful and loving and there is no fear. If you've never tried it, I heartily recommend it. All you have to do is stop, breathe and focus on this moment right now.

The fear busting check-list:

- Step outside your comfort zone a short pace, often. Feel not only the fear but the exhilaration and the sense of achievement.

- Name your fears aloud and see them for what they are; just like the fictitious bogeymen under the bed: the mysterious figure in the shadows, just a dressing gown on the back of the door. None of them have actually come to fruition.

- Spend time with those you love and trust your whole attention to them in the moments you are with them.

- Contemplate: be in the present moment with God – at any and all moments.

- Meditate: explore your truth with God, often.

In other faith traditions, the word meditation is used for the practice Christians call contemplation; in the remainder of this book, where I use the word contemplation it also describes this kind of meditation.

Circle of God
Surround me
Protect, Empower
And Shield me
Now and always. Amen.

5

A Healthy Body

"Do you not know that your body is a temple of the Holy Spirit" 1 Corinthians 6:19

In the West, we have become completely fixated on the outward appearance of the body and yet almost oblivious to the vital part it plays in our emotional, psychological and spiritual well-being. As I walk down any high street, I see the two polarised body issues; ultra-thinness and obesity. Both strike me as a cry for help, a silent declaration of self-loathing; an externalising of emotional insecurity and a desire for something more in our lives to fill the void that we vainly chuck our consumerist items into, only to have them swallowed up by the emptiness.

We are teaching our young to value themselves according to their thinness rather than their uniqueness and setting in motion a fast approaching catastrophe in doing so. Our media constantly bombards us with digitally perfected images of women and men to which we are told we should aspire, yet to which we know we cannot attain. This is a manipulative marketing strategy which leaves few people completely unaffected. The biggest lie behind the whole media/fashion/celebrity/marketing industry campaign, is that we can be perfect. When I asked a fifteen-year-old girl what 'perfect' meant, she told me, "It's being thin, pretty and having great hair and clothes". All externals, all skin deep. When I asked her about the bad effects of extreme dieting on hair, she replied, "It doesn't matter; you can get your hair fixed."

I don't only blame industry, however; some of the responsibility has to be laid at the door of the Church for its sin of omission where the body is concerned. Unlike many Eastern faiths, modern Western Christianity rarely shows any real consideration for the body, except to encourage caution and modesty wherever it's concerned. It started with some Greek philosophers; they made a clear distinction between the body (weak, bad) and the mind/spirit (strong, good).While the Greeks appreciated the beauty of the human body and often celebrated the naked form, the New Testament was written by Greek *Jews* who passed on not only the notion of separating mind/spirit and body but also Jewish taboos about the body. Of course, they could have had no idea how things would pan out in a couple of thousand years.

Consequently, in all too many churches, we find the Christianity being taught has no specifically physical dimension to its practice and no real notion of the body being in partnership with the spirit. It allows three basic postures; sitting, standing and kneeling (although the latter's largely gone out of fashion in our sedentary society). Buddhism, Taoism and other Eastern faiths have developed systems such as Yoga and Tai Chi, which not only train the body and the mind but include the spirit and emotions, too,

Even though, throughout the ages, there have been those who have championed the importance of the body, what too many people experience is a weak, negative message about the body. It's not important unless it's leading you down a path the Church doesn't approve of. It's temporary; we won't need it in 'the next life' and therefore it's disposable and not worthy of respect. It's inextricably linked with sexuality and the Church is crippled in its approach to human sexuality.

This is a curious development for a faith which actually has the body at the centre of its foundation! The living body, the suffering body, the dying body, the resurrected body. The stories surrounding Jesus involve healing sick bodies, foot washing, foot kissing, feeding hungry bodies, clothing naked ones and bringing dead bodies back to life. They involve the notion of a

God who made and loves our bodies even more than the most amazing creatures and plants of our planet. So there is plenty of material for a more healthy, positive approach to human bodies within Christian spirituality. There is a need for more people who have a more positive view of the body to speak up within the Church.

Our ancient Celtic ancestors would have been puzzled by our denial of the importance of our bodies to our spiritual lives. The Celts knew their acute need for their bodies and for healthy bodies, as they worked the land and survived bitter winters. They understood their own procreative cycles through their connectedness with the land and the rest of creation. The body was seen as precious and holy as it housed the soul. The appeal of Celtic Christianity today is in no small way due to its physicality; that it is grounded in the earth; it expresses creativity, productivity, sensuality and the unpredictability of life. In his amazing book 'Anam Cara' John O'Donahue draws out the significance of the Celtic approach to the body in our modern day setting;

"It is in and through your body that your soul becomes real for you. Your body is the home of your soul on earth"

God is in the ground beneath my feet, the air I breathe, the sky above me. God moves in all the creatures of the earth, changes in the seasons, the wheel of the year. God is in the pauses between the words within my thoughts. In touching nature, I touch God. In physical creativity, I mirror God's creativity. In repetitive, physical labour, I echo the heartbeat of the creator and I know I am alive.

Jesus gave importance to the body and its needs in his teaching and actions. He fell out with some of the religious leaders of his day because he flouted religious laws about the Sabbath in order to heal someone who was sick and again by not chastising his disciples when they picked wheat, crushed it in their hands and ate it on a Sabbath (thus breaking rules about labouring on the Sabbath) because they were hungry. "The Sabbath was made for man, not man for the Sabbath" (Mark 2:27) was probably one of his most provocative teachings in his day. The gospels are full of Jesus' preoccupation with the bodily needs of others; feeding the 5,000, healing the sick, turning water into wine at a wedding, putting his arms around children and weeping over the physical loss of a friend.

Most powerful of all for me, is his institution of what we now call communion. This central act is absolutely physical, absolutely about the body; his body and our bodies. In his last meal with his friends, he gave himself to them as he shared the bread and wine and told them to consume him; to make him part of them. In this profound yet simple ritual lies an intimacy that is breathtaking. In our modern day ritual we remember Jesus; we put him back together and make him physically real and physically part of us, as we share communion. We can only do this with our bodies; they are the means by which we become united with Jesus.

I sometimes wonder whether, the reduction of communion down to tasteless wafers and sips of fairly unpalatable communion wine has in some way obscured the physicality of the Church's central ritual. By taking away any sense of pleasure in the eating and drinking, perhaps we have made this a perfunctory, symbolic act instead of the enriching meal it was intended to be. One of the most beautiful prayers in modern Anglican liturgy is this prayer of access from the Church in Wales:

Lord Jesus Christ
You draw and welcome us,
Emptied of pride and hungry for your grace,
To this your kingdom's feast.
Nowhere can we find the food
for which our souls cry out,
but here, Lord, at your table.

Invigorate and nourish us, good Lord;
That in and through this bread and wine
Your love may meet us
And your life complete us
In the power and glory of your kingdom. Amen.

Whilst a priest in the Church in Wales, I prepared a group of seven young women for confirmation and when it came to the practice for making first communion, they all agreed that the wafers were horrible. The line in the prayer "Nowhere can we find the food for which our souls cry out but here your Lord at your table" rose up to hit me in the face: we were saying such powerful words and yet serving up such unappealing elements! If the richness of our spiritual beliefs is to be properly expressed, it needs to be manifested in a correspondingly rich physical reality. It is through our bodies that we experience the richness of life and this should surely include our spiritual life. I shared this insight with the PCC and as a result, we began to use bread and wine that was accessible to everyone, regardless of dietary needs, and also tasted good!

I remember the first time I was invited to attend a pagan hand fasting (wedding); when it came to sharing the cup and plate, there was a good wine and in place of bland wafers, there were cakes and I thought how mean and reserved the Church appeared by comparison! We could, surely, extend our efforts to producing something that inspired the taste buds, rather than sent people away from the altar wincing at the taste of the wine and trying discreetly to get the wafer off the roof of their mouths! There is also the issue of making this most precious physical ritual accessible to all, in spite of dietary needs. Our hospitality fails utterly if we force coeliacs and alcoholics to announce that they are different at this most holy and intimate moment of communion, which is nothing less than union with God and the community of the Church.

It is hospitality that colours the Celtic spiritual life from start to finish. Hospitality is a spiritual act; it is a cornerstone of the Celtic way of life. Sadly, it has been lost or at least forgotten to many in these islands. No Celt would have dreamt of not offering warmth, food and shelter to guests and visitors, yet so often when visiting a house these days, our hosts can barely bother themselves to switch off the television set to give us their attention! The Celtic Christian saw welcoming strangers as welcoming Christ. To spurn, abuse or reject hospitality was a serious offence. Hospitality was not just an act of physical provision but an offering from the heart. Nowadays, people mostly experience bought board and lodging and food served up with little love and not true hospitality and we are the poorer for this. Rublev's famous icon of the trinity reminds us that hospitality is at the heart of God. The setting of the icon is the Old Testament story of the visit of The Lord under the guise of three strangers to Abraham and Sarah. The image is of three angels seated around a table, the angels are understood to be the three members of the trinity. However, the perspective has been cleverly reversed, so that the table gets wider as it goes away from you, rather than narrower and this has the effect of inviting you into the picture; welcoming you to the table; welcoming you into the hospitality and heart of the Godhead.

Jesus' last act with his friends, his giving of the act of communion, is a reminder of the generosity, love and passion of God for people; it is a call for us to accept the hospitality of the Godhead.

Of course, this meal is also a remembrance of the suffering and death of Jesus. This humiliating, barbaric and excruciating part of the story of the life of Jesus cannot be avoided. Indeed, it is the pivot point of the Christian message. It is physically that Jesus declares his commitment to his principles, his teaching, his God and it is physically that he pays for them. It is through the agony of his body, that we know the agony of his heart and can believe in the totality of his love for friends and strangers alike. It is through his body pinioned to a cross, that we learn the message 'it stops here!' The cycle of abuse and revenge must be brought to an end; healing and forgiveness must triumph and love must be at the centre of all life.

Yet the story has one more role for the body; that of resurrection. Even in this most spiritual of aspects, it is the body of Jesus that is central. It is vital that his friends and followers see him; experience his presence. He must physically demonstrate that life is stronger than death and light overcomes darkness. He must stand among them and show them the way through his recognisable appearance in order for them to understand that healing and life in all its fullness is being offered to them. This physical relationship of compassion and healing is extended to the world around us through our bodies today, as so succinctly expressed in the song 'Touching Place' by John Bell and Graham Maule:

"To the lost Christ shows his face;
To the unloved he gives his embrace;
To those who cry in pain or disgrace
Christ makes with his friends a touching place"

Perhaps it is not only our indoctrination that leads us to largely ignore the body within the Christian spiritual life; perhaps it is our discomfort with sexuality. A couple of years ago at a baptism in one of my churches, a young female guest appeared clearly dressed for a party. She was pretty, had a lovely figure and was well groomed. She was wearing what I can only describe as a crocheted, white dress; it was as much made up of holes as it was fabric, with a plunging neckline and a high hem, it was very revealing. She was not inhibited about her attire, she was perfectly natural and comfortable and she looked beautiful. Yet I couldn't help wondering whether her attire was in some way 'wrong' for church and also what the men in the congregation were making of her. I was challenged by this reaction within me. Was she not God's beautiful handiwork? Why was her beauty and sexuality somehow inappropriate in church? Was our de-sexualising of everyone and everything within our liturgy impoverishing us in some way? Is it not our sexual energy that we use to imbue our liturgy with passion?

We have been given this gift of a body; it is ours in which to live and experience the world and we need to accept and love it just as it is. This is against everything that the media is telling us but that's because they want to sell us products. Your spirit needs this body to exist here on earth; your mind relies on the information and nourishment it receives from your body; your emotions reside and experience themselves in your body. Any trauma or change to the body affects the mind, spirit and emotions equally. Our bodies are the vehicles through which we touch the earth and each other; they are the place where human and divine meet; they are the means by which we achieve the physical expression of love.

It is surely, then, a spiritual imperative to respect and care for our bodies. Going to work when you are sick, pushing your body beyond its physical capabilities, over eating, under eating, over consumption of alcohol or caffeine: these are all abuse of the body! Too often we give in to the bullies who wish us all to conform to the same specification; to live the way they do, to work the way they do, to reinforce their sense of importance or beauty or relevance or rightness. To prop up their overdeveloped and fragile egos. The airbrushed images that bombard us through the media, trick our minds and lead us to look at ourselves as less than beautiful; less than worthy. We are constantly told that there is only one form of beauty and it is thin, young and enhanced through cosmetic procedures. We might as well be clones! The media seems to wish nothing more than a procession of clothes horses that are uniform and bland without an ounce of originality or personality.

Your body expresses you; informs your personality, marks you out as unique, is the point of recognition between you and others. Not only does it deserve the respect of a balanced diet, sufficient exercise, adequate shelter, physical and sexual expression; it is also one part of the answer to achieving inner peace and a quiet mind. It is a crucial part of your journey to self discovery and self expression.

The body has a memory and a 'mind'; it receives messages of trauma or pleasure, fear or happiness and responds with immediacy. If you have ever seen a wild animal hit by a car yet get up and run away, you will have seen the body's instinctive response. The proverbial 'headless chicken' reacting to the nervous and chemical messages surging through its system. The body doesn't only respond in emergencies; when the mind is playing with its negative thoughts and stimulating negative feelings, the body will respond with posture and how it processes the chemicals and stimulants generated by the brain when the mood changes; it will feed into the negative cycle.

We've all heard of the 'exercise improves mood' theory because it's right; we know that exercising the body results in the production of endorphins that make us feel more positive. We all also know how eating certain foods improve our mood; some because of their properties (e.g. chocolate) and some because of their associations or consistency; so called 'comfort foods'.

There is more to the link between the body and mood, however. We can all see another person's mood via their body language. We recognise the following emotions when they are physically expressed: vulnerable, miserable, proud, angry, without a word being spoken. We see the emotion being person-ified in the body. If someone is vulnerable, s/he will sink in the middle to protect the stomach, the shoulders will come forward to do the same for the chest and the chin drop to cover the throat, the legs close together from the knees up, to protect the groin.

We don't actively think through the process of adopting this posture; it's instinctive. Likewise, our reading of the posture is instinctive.

We can use these instinctive reactions consciously with remarkably good effect! If you are not feeling confident, try this exercise:

Stand or sit with your feet hip-width apart, feet facing straight ahead, tailbone tucked slightly underneath you. Straighten your spine by lifting it from the diaphragm (just below your rib cage) let your arms hang straight at your sides and tell your shoulders to soften (yes; telling your body to do something works!). Tip your chin slightly towards your chest and imagine that your head is being held up by two strings tied to two invisible bolts just above your ears. Look straight ahead.

How do you feel when you stand in this confident pose?

Now, imagine you've just won a quiz, competition or deal and shake a triumphant fist in front of you and say 'Yes!'

How do you feel now?

Move one foot a step behind the other and turn the toes so that your feet are pointing 10 to 2 on a clock face. Shift your weight onto your back leg (hip if you're sitting) and bend the knee slightly on the front leg, pushing the corresponding shoulder forward, so that your upper body is at the same angle as your hips. Place your hands on your hips and stick your chest out. Tilt your head slightly to one side.

How does this pose make you feel?

By using the signals of our body, we can make a difference to our mood.

We can use our face to make the change even more noticeable. Actors know this; they use it to create the emotions of the characters they are playing.

Dig out a photo or yourself in which you look happy, proud or contented. Do this exercise *without* a mirror. (If you can't find a photo of yourself, use one of someone else).

Study the face in the photo; what angle is the head at? Is the brow furrowed or clear? What are the eyebrows doing? Are the eyes piercing or soft in focus? What shape has the mouth taken? The cheeks, nose, jaw?

Now copy the facial expression; look at the photo and think the shape of the brow, eyebrows, mouth etc onto your face and move them as you feel ready.

When you have the facial expression, put the photo down and explore how your body wants to respond to match your face. Can you find a phrase that matches how your face and body feel? e.g. 'This is great!' 'So peaceful!' 'Happy bunny!' etc.

Take your time over these exercises; they might feel strange at first but come back to them frequently until they take effect more easily.

You might not have noticed but I suspect that negative thoughts and feelings have subsided while you've been engrossed in these exercises.

Christ go before me to guide me
Behind me to protect me
And beside me as my friend
This day and always. Amen.

6

The Body in Prayer

Breathing is central to the contemplative state; breathing is both our way of remaining alive and our means to control the functions of our body and mind. Whether we breathe in a short, fast, shallow way or deeply and slowly profoundly affects how our bodies function and how we feel. Many of us do not take enough deep, slow breaths and are, therefore, not taking in enough oxygen to function to our fullest capacity or even to give our voices enough power to reach across a room or stay strong to the end of a sentence. Breathing affects the rate of our hearts and the rate of our hearts influences our sense of calm or anxiety and is itself affected by those same feelings. Breath and breathing are themes that run through Christian spirituality; the breath of God is one description for the Holy Spirit. In John's gospel, Jesus gives the Holy Spirit to his disciples by breathing on them. Breath is life; to breathe is to live.

It is possible to slow your own heart rate; in fact it is easier to slow your own heart rate than to stop the chattering thoughts in your mind or change the churning feeling in your solar plexus. Breathing is the key to slowing your heart rate.

Exercise

Place your hand over your heart and close your eyes. Breathe deeply in through your nose to the count of four, making sure you are breathing from your diaphragm (your chest should not move but your stomach should rise and fall). Hold the breath for a count of two and then breathe out through your mouth to a count of four. Repeat this twice more.

Now continue to breathe deeply and slowly, in through the nose and out through the mouth to the count of four (do not hold your breath in between). As you breathe in, visualise the air as pink, flowing in through your nasal passages, down into your lungs and washing over your heart.

As well as your heart slowing, a calmer feeling comes to the solar plexus and the mind becomes stiller. This is a useful tool in situations of anxiety! It is also central to meditation; breathing deeply and slowly is essential to enter into the meditative state; it is the first point of focus but once we are calm we can let the breathing take care of itself and focus elsewhere.

Body posture

Sitting is the new kneeling. What I mean by this statement is that, in the last couple of decades, the posture for contemplation has often been defined thus: sit on a dining style chair with both feet flat on the ground, your spine straight but relaxed and your hands in your lap.

This is a welcome progression from kneeling, hands together and eyes shut, however it is still a prescribed posture. For someone like me with a dodgy back and short legs it's uncomfortable verging on painful. It doesn't feel natural for my body and so I am simply conforming to something prescribed by someone else who finds it helpful. You might find it the perfect posture in which case, stick with it!

There are many postures for contemplation, possibly as many as there are people. Rather than copying a formula, we need to explore the truth that our bodies communicate to us. Is lying down or standing up best? Sitting cross-legged or sinking on a sofa? Does repetitive movement help? Are you given to dance; to move like the Shakers or Whirling Dervishes? How does your body communicate with the Divine?

There is even more to the body's role than finding the right posture or movement for meditation, however. It can serve to focus the mind and bring you into the divine presence in the present moment through its demanding of your attention. Just as the body distracts us from concentration through discomfort or pain, so it can bring us into focus through demanding our willpower. This is why Eastern meditation involves postures; the full lotus position demands the mind use its full willpower to keep the body in the correct position and under exactly the right tension, thus freeing it from incessant thoughts. The posture is practiced; the mind and body must work in unity to achieve it, thus freeing the unconscious mind to the process of meditation. I'm not, however, suggesting you rush off and tie yourself up in an agonising position; just using it as an example! It could quickly become the next new kneeling, even if you can achieve it safely.

Other Eastern postures give more clues. The arms and hands are extended into positions that add just enough stress to the body to focus the mind. For example, 'Fire Palm' where the arms are extended straight in front of the body but without locking the elbows, the hands are raised as if in front of a fire or pushing against a wall. This can be done seated, cross-legged on the floor or standing. It can be done standing in 'Bear' position: with the feet shoulder-width apart and the legs straight but the knees not locked or in 'Riding on a horse' position: with the legs wide apart, the feet facing forward and the seat lowered to a sitting position. I'd recommend you try it first in 'Bear' position! Another arm and hand position will be more familiar to those from the Christian tradition; 'Heaven palm' has the arms extended to either side, elbows dropped and hands facing upwards. The position adopted by priests presiding at communion services and also by charismatic Christians during worship.

I have found that the tension and focus demanded by adopting such arm postures does two things. Firstly, it brings me quickly into the present moment and thereby aids the stilling of my mind. Secondly, something less expected happens; as I maintain this position, my sense of my body wanes until I arrive at a place where I barely feel it. Yet my mind remains focussed and still. It is as if my unconscious mind is free of restraint and about its natural business of unity with the Divine and all creation. In this state, images can freely move into my mind and my awareness of the immanence of the whole of creation, the link between my spirit and all spirit is almost tangible. The odd thought may wander in but the power of the experience continues within the unconscious.

Coming out of this state needs to be done gently and slowly; listening to the needs of the body, mind, emotions and spirit. It is likely that your heart rate will have slowed and as you will have been breathing more deeply, you will have taken in more oxygen. Become aware of your body; when you feel your arms more normally, move them back to your sides and rest them there. Be aware of how your body feels. Take some moments to relocate your mind within your body, think some thoughts. Do not move suddenly and when you do, do so gently and slowly until you feel you are back in your normal physical state.

Spirit of God
Dwell in my heart and inspire my feelings.
Spirit of God
Move in my mind and direct my thoughts.
Spirit of God
Touch my lips and guide my words. Amen.

7

Pain and Contemplation

Physical pain brings us into the present moment in a way we'd rather not experience it. It is important to distinguish between two types of pain; Acute pain, which is the result of a recent injury or illness (e.g. a broken bone or a hernia) and Chronic pain, the type that continues long after an initial injury or illness (e.g. arthritis or ME). Acute pain needs to be accepted and respected; it tells us of a need to slow down, to take care and to show our bodies the love and understanding they need to heal. When we're in an acute condition, we might want to simply see our patient wait for healing as our prayer, if we do not have the energy or concentration for mediation. Sometimes we need to cut ourselves some slack; be kind to ourselves and take it easy. Escaping into a good film or sleeping may be the best thing for us. If you want to try a healing meditation, try the section marked * in the list below.

In the case of chronic pain, we have to encourage, motivate ourselves to live as full a life as possible and contemplation can be an aid in this. Some tips for contemplating when experiencing chronic pain:

- Don't adopt the pose; the new kneeling. Find the position that you are comfortable in and in which you feel the least pain. Even if you are in a contemplative group, do not feel inhibited and sit in pain. I have often lain on the floor during group contemplation because I have back pain and no-one has been bothered. In fact, I often find other back pain sufferers take it as a cue to give themselves permission to do the same!

- When you bring your full focus to a point at the start of contemplation, make it outside of your own body; across the room or out of the window. When you focus, direct all your energy at that point of focus; imagine your breath is travelling towards the image and follow your gaze with your energy.

If you wish, try this healing visualisation: *

- When you have achieved the state of being fully in the present moment, breathe in and as you do so, visualise the air you breathe as orange or gold. Imagine the air flowing down into your body and circulating over the areas of pain, gathering the pain into itself and leaving your body as you exhale.

Chronic pain often leads to the holding of tension in the body and so further pain is caused in other areas because of tense posture. A simple relaxation technique can help here, as can gentle yoga, tai chi or keep fit stretches.

A relaxation technique

(This is just one example plenty are available in books and online and many recorded ones to guide you through a relaxation).

Lie as flat as you can without feeling pain or discomfort, use a pillow or cushion under your head. If you need to bend your legs, place a pillow under your knees so that your legs can relax.

Take a deep breath (from the diaphragm) in through your nose to the count of four – hold the breath to the count of two – breathe out through the mouth to the count of four. Repeat twice more. Keep your breathing steady and slow.

Now focus your attention on your feet and say (either aloud or in your head to yourself) 'My feet are feeling heavy; my feet are feeling warm'.

Next focus on your lower legs and say 'My lower legs are feeling heavy; my lower legs are feeling warm'.

Repeat this for each part of your body until you have relaxed yourself from the toes to the top of your head.

Now rest in this relaxed position for at least 10 minutes. When you are ready, take a deep breath in and let out a long, slow sigh. Repeat twice more. Gently wiggle your toes and then your fingers. Become aware of your legs, torso and arms, neck and head. When you are ready, roll onto your side and carefully get up.

Emotional pain

Acute emotional pain is debilitating and dreadful. I would rather suffer the worst back pain I have ever had than emotional pain. I know others who would say the same. It is difficult to find rest or respite from emotional pain and the way it plays on the mind. In a state of acute emotional pain, it is almost impossible to contemplate in a way that brings any sense of peace.

Here are some things I have found helpful:

- Emotional pain is felt in a particular area of the body. In my case, I experience it in the solar plexus. I have known people who experience it elsewhere; the chest is also a common place to feel emotional pain.

When we are suffering, we tend to focus on the area of our body where the pain is; move your focus to another area of the body, perhaps your throat or forehead or the your pelvic girdle and concentrate hard on this place until you are fully present in that part of your body. When we take ourselves away from the physical expression of the pain, we help to relieve the mental anguish, too. This exercise needs practice; we have to combat our tendency to sink into our psychological suffering. If you practise, you will find you can shift your focus around your body to calm places away from wherever the suffering is; if the chattering mind is the problem, move to the pelvic girdle (your strong base), if the solar plexus is the problem, move to the head and so on.

When you are able to operate from a safer place and set of emotions, you can reach into the present moment and top up your spiritual energy from the Divine.

* Meridian tapping

It is possible to raise the mood and energy by this technique. I was taught it when I was suffering from acute anxiety, owing to a situation in which I was being harassed by someone with serious mental health issues. I found it calmed, focussed, distracted and energised me. At the time I didn't care whether it was hocus pocus or not, now I'm convinced it isn't because it worked!

There are two parts to the process; the places to tap and the things you say to yourself. I would advise that you read through the instructions below once before practising.

I would advise against practising meridian tapping after 6pm in the evening, as its energy boosting effects may make it difficult for you to get to sleep!

For anxiety, depression and low energy, you tap 9 times with the fingertips of the three longest fingers of your right hand (reverse right and left throughout if you are left handed):

The top of your head

While you are tapping the top of your head, you say aloud to yourself what you need to hear e.g. 'I am anxious/low/ distressed but I totally love and accept myself. I am already feeling a bit better and I am going to feel even better now'.

Then you tap 9 times:

Between your eyebrows

Beside your right eye

Above your top lip

The right collar bone (just below neck)

The rib cage adjacent to your left elbow

Your left thumb and finger nails in turn (finishing with little finger)

9 times at the place on your hand between the finger bones of your left ring and little finger and then sing aloud a line of a song (can be a nursery rhyme, happy birthday or something meaningful to you) repeat this tapping of hand 9 times and singing twice more.

Then, without moving your head, look down to your left and then down to your right, followed by moving your eyes in a clockwise circle.

Repeat the whole process twice more.

Now you may well feel able to contemplate a little, or do any of the other things you wish with your time. It is important not to expect too much of yourself when you are experiencing emotional pain; take the right amount of rest necessary; our very suffering is, in itself, a reaching out to God.

Breath of God

Surround me

Light of God

Fill me

Love of God

Heal me. Amen.

8

A Free Spirit

Unlike the mind, body and emotions, we do not need to train the spirit; we simply need to free it to operate. If we persevere with the work on our minds, emotions and bodies, we will allow the space for our spirits to speak to us and to inform us and bring us the peace and integrity we long for. Too often, the spirit is suppressed and dominated by the mind and emotions; starved of food and daylight, it longs to bring its gifts to us but is only able to do so in our dreams because we shut ourselves off from its truth.

Yet, the spirit can be released, recognised, speak to us at any moment; if we dare to allow it. For many, music and artistic expression are two key ways of allowing the spirit freedom to roam and dance. For others, being in the midst of nature; whether in the countryside, at the coast, in the garden or looking through a window. Music certainly has a unique way of expressing deep truths, feelings and hopes; of all the arts, it communicates with the Spirit most profoundly because it touches our bodies, minds and emotions equally, making them open to our spirits. Songs, which combine the power of thought in words, the power of emotions in melody and the physical power of rhythm, allow our spirits to bring out our aspirations and hopes, to challenge us to explore and fulfil them. When the mind, emotions and body have been nurtured and heard, they will free the spirit to lead us; to take control, to express who we are fully. Many people have sought to find a sense of peace through alcohol or recreational drugs but the truth is, the real peace we seek is already within us and simply needs to be allowed to be. By finding our places and activities of spiritual release, we find our sense of inner peace.

When we come to contemplate, we offer our attention to our spirit; we give our spirit the space to express its divine nature and draw us close to the Divine. We step out of so-called time and into eternity in the present moment; the only real time.

Spirituality goes beyond religion; what I mean by this is that religion is organised, it has rules and regulations; it's organised by people, albeit people who seek to express the will of the Divine through their religious codes, practices and rituals. The life of the spirit is linked directly to the Divine; it perceives divine truth and wisdom directly, if we let it. Religion has sprung up (since time immemorial) and become dominant because people do not pay attention to their spiritual dimension. Jesus talked of God as being as close as a parent; at hand to respond to requests, intimately involved in our lives. Yet, we continue to push the Divine to a more comfortable distance; insist that he or she is waiting for us to make mistakes and demanding that we grovel and degrade ourselves because it's easier and less demanding of us in our individual response. We'd rather be told what to do by another human being than listen to the Divine directly.

"God is Spirit and his worshippers must worship in spirit and in truth." Jesus says in John 4:24 (NIV)

Religion deals with rights and wrongs, positives and negatives, morality and immorality, virtues and sins. Our spiritual lives can lead us to transcend all of these things and be guided instead by wisdom, truth and love into a state of integrity, that includes our bodies, minds and emotions. A state of peace; a state where we can find a quiet mind.

The Celts had a different concept of time from modern day society. For the Celts, time was not linear but circular. It didn't start at one date and progress forward to another but went round in cycles and circles, just as the seasons of the earth do. The plants of the earth shoot and grow and seed and die only to shoot again; we and the other creatures do the same. What is eternal and unchanging, is spirit; Divine spirit; our spirit; the planet's spirit; creation's spirit. All joined, all one, all eternal.

The Celts also had a notion of 'thin places' where the veil between the physical world and the spiritual one were thin; places where it is easier to feel close to the eternal, the Divine and to those who have died and moved fully into the world of spirit. There was also a time of the year when the veil was believed to thin; now called Halloween but originally Samhain in Irish and Calan Gaeaf in Welsh. Perhaps there are 'thin' people, too; people in whom we can see the Divine more easily; who are a gateway between the two dimensions?

The Celtic heritage is ours to explore and experience; it was so nearly crushed by formal Christianity in the dark ages but it survived, underground and through poetry, story and song and is regaining ground again within both Christian and Pagan circles. It is a spirituality strongly linked to the land here in the British Isles; it is in our soil and our water; in our blood and our collective memory.

When I was a child, I believed my soul was an oval shaped object, rather like an Easter egg. I wasn't sure where it was located, just that it *was*. Perhaps I was an odd child; I can't remember a time when I didn't know there was a 'God', a divine, caring presence who was intimately close to me. Now I see that my childish notion of the shape of the soul might have had something in it. I suspect that the soul or spirit, as I prefer to call it, is not inside the body but the body inside the spirit. That would, indeed, make the spirit a sort of oval, encompassing the body. The body being inside the spirit would account for the spiritual connection between human beings and the rest of creation; we can sort of 'squidge' into each other, overlap, join up, even! It would also link in with concepts of auras and energy held for millennia in various parts of the world. Perhaps you, too, had spiritual instincts as a child but hid them away as you grew up. Returning to what you knew as a child can be revealing and spiritually liberating.

There's something else, I suspect about spirit; and that is that it can exist in more than one place at a time. That it is in the physical world with our bodies and also in the spiritual dimension or 'heaven'. Or to put it another way, the spiritual dimension exists side by side with the physical one and we live in both at the same time; our physical selves can't see the spiritual dimension because we are not equipped with the faculties in our bodies and brains but our spirits can perceive it. Like the ancient Celts, I think that spirit is eternal; it is the part of us that goes on continuously throughout what we understand as time. I wait in fascination to learn where quantum physics takes us in its study of dimensions; perhaps it will prove the ancient Celts right!

9

Dreams, Visions and Voices

The Bible, along with many other religious texts, has God communicating through dreams, visions and voices. In the Christian tradition of the Western world, we've become a little more prosaic over such communication. The cause hasn't been helped by overzealous, attention-seekers who insist that they are God's new best friend with messages for all and sundry. The subject is also fraught with the difficulties surrounding the issue of religious psychosis. The scepticism born out of increased understanding of mental health and the debunking of charlatans has led to many being cautious about their own spiritual experiences. None of us wants to be labelled 'mad'. Yet spiritual experiences continue to happen even amongst the most rational, down to earth people. There is nothing 'supernatural' about spiritual experiences; they are utterly natural but we don't always have the language to explain them. In our spirit, we are linked together, to the Divine and to the whole of creation; what Jung called the 'collective unconscious'. We perceive things, see things, hear things that we cannot account for with our 5 senses but we utterly know to have occurred. I want to share three of my own experiences here, to illustrate what I mean. They may well resonate with your own experiences.

Visions

One night, a few years ago, as I was meditating, the image of a woman's face flashed into my mind's eye. It was clear and unmistakable; I knew the woman, although I couldn't recall her name. She had been an inmate in the prison where I was chaplain some months before. The image was so striking that, even after a night's sleep, I couldn't shake the experience from my mind. At work the next morning, I saw the same woman walking onto the landing of a wing; she had been brought into prison again. I asked an officer for the woman's name and then inquired whether she was ok. 'Why, what do you know? Is there something wrong?' he was a little panicked. 'No, I just wondered.' I replied. Well I could hardly say 'I had a vision of her last night', could I? He'd have thought I was a total weirdo! Later that morning, I found myself walking towards the same woman on a corridor; she was being escorted by a nurse. I took the opportunity to stop and say, 'Hi! Are you ok?' She looked astounded and said, 'Yes! No! I don't know!' The nurse winked to me to indicate that she'd follow the situation up and later came and told me that the woman had admitted that she had very big problems but now that she'd admitted to them, she could get help.

Of course, for each of the times when I have been able to make sense of such an experience, there have been others where there seems to be no rhyme nor reason behind my seeing or knowing that something is wrong; nothing that I am able to do to change or help a situation. There are times when we do not understand our experiences and our only choice is to accept that things are as they are.

Dreams

I have many dreams that I remember; I am one of the minority of people who dreams in colour. However, occasionally I have dreams that mark themselves out because of the quality of the images and the style of the content. One such dream, with its total cinematic, high definition, surround sound quality took me by surprise.

I was standing in a field in an Eastern country with a number of soldiers whose commanding officer was a woman I know.

Beside us was a mound of dead bodies and a little further down the field, a derelict, wooden church. The commanding officer was instructing the troops to move the bodies into the church and set fire to it. I protested loudly and with great passion that it was wrong to burn the church. Eventually, I conceded that her plan was the right one and necessary.

I emailed a therapist friend to ask for some guidance in understanding a hidden, deeper meaning in the dream. He obliged with some suggestions, which I explored.

A few days later, I was having lunch with a fellow cleric from a neighbouring parish and recounted the dream to her. She listened with a stunned expression and when I'd finished, she recounted a dream she'd had two days before, in which she'd been trying to persuade people who were 'living dead' to leave a burning church but they refused to do so.

I emailed my therapist friend again. He said that while the dead, un-dead and burning churches are not uncommon in dreams, what on earth was the Spirit doing in our neck of the world?

Sometimes our dreams aren't just a way of downloading our experiences but can actually guide us; lead us to explore our deeper awareness and act to change and heal ourselves and help those around us to do the same.

Voices

Earlier, I mentioned a time when I was being harassed in my home by a stranger with mental health problems. It was a time when I experienced great fear that kept me from sleeping and functioning properly. I went away for a few days to find some sanctuary to a place I knew I could sleep and be away from the fear. While there I experienced an acute attack of anxiety. I refused to give in to it; I dealt with it by using some of the methods I have mentioned in the section on feelings. When I had managed to let go of the fear and the anxiety had left me, I was exhausted and lay on the bed, empty of energy and thought. As clear as a bell, a voice spoke in my head, not my voice, not an external voice that I heard with my ears, but a voice of 'someone' that directly entered my head. It said, "That's the last thing you have to let go of; the fear. Now will you let me be your parent?"

I laid there in stunned silence before offering the courtesy of 'Ok, thank you!' I'm not going to try to explain where the voice came from or how I heard it; but hear it, I did.

When I have shared my experiences with others, I have found that I am not alone; many people are having these kinds of spiritual experiences; perfectly ordinary people, Church people, people of other faiths, agnostic people. What is missing in so many situations is the environment to share the stories, to affirm their reality.

10

Finding Thin Places

You may already have special places where you feel at peace, calm, in the present moment; close to the Divine. You may think you haven't but perhaps you haven't recognised them in this way. Try spending a moment recalling places where you felt those emotions; that sense of calm; perhaps these are your thin places? They may be close at hand; your garden, a local church-yard or park or they may be somewhere you need to travel to reach, a special stretch of coastline, a particular valley or a mountain. If you can't think of anywhere that makes you feel this way, perhaps it's time to discover somewhere? To begin with, you could try some places that lots of other people have called 'thin places' for many years. There are websites and books dedicated to introducing such places. Here are some of mine, for starters:

Llangasty tal y llyn, Powys Wales
Ynyslas Reserve Borth, Ceredigion, West Wales
Pennant Melangell, Llangynog, Powys, Wales
Neist Point, the Isle of Skye, Scotland
Nine Ladies stone circle, Stanton Moor, Derbyshire, England
Glendalough, County Waterford, Ireland

For me, mountains, hills and water play a significant part in creating a thin place. Where they come together in places such as Llangasty and Glendalough, the effect is immensely powerful. It's no accident that they were inhabited by early Celtic Christians and were sites of ancient pagan spirituality before that. It is perhaps easiest to explain the depth of the experience of thin places through poetry.

Llangasty
Out across the lake
Your spirit flies, hovers.
Holiness reflected in the twin,
Grey-blue mirrors of your nature.
I marvel at your stillness.
Swans glide across your surface
At home within the flow
Of your life-force;
Held between your twin presence
As air touches water.
Swifts soar and dive amongst
The currents of your breath
And I, in stillness, can only
Wonder at your closeness
As you envelope me, also.
3.6.07

So many demands for our time and attention can crowd in and drain us, knocking us off balance with our natural spiritual rhythm. Going away to a thin place, whether for a few hours or a few days, provides the space and absence of distraction both of which can enhance our spiritual lives and help us to regain balance within our lives. When I return to Llangasty each year for my retreat, it is a homecoming; a spiritual homecoming, as well as a physical one to a retreat house of comfort and nurture. Spending time in such a place enables me to rest, to breathe in the peace and power and to grow in insight. The following poem is about this retreat experience where I spend time in both the crypt chapel and outdoors, beside the lake.

The Twin Journey
Hidden in this tomb
This hiding place of the soul

Invisible to the people who
Go about their day.
Footsteps overhead
And voices passing.
I am hidden
Secreted in your womb.
I tunnel inwards
With the intensity of your power.
Just you and me
In the laden stillness
Charged with your energy.
Later, much later, I will leave this inward journey
For a while
And travel ever outward
Into the expanse of creation
Let my oneness with all else
Expand and travel in the air
Amidst the damsels and the moths
Out into this vast
Yet intimate universe.
15.5.08

When I return from my retreat, I bring the sense of peace and wonder back with me; a hermit returning from an inward journey, a lamp held high to shine on the path ahead of her. The visits to my thin places help me to restore balance in my life; the balance between work and rest, private and public, creativity and the mundane. I hold these places and the experiences they bring me in my head and I can visualise myself there on the lakeside at Llangasty or the shore at Ynyslas at any moment and remember, put back together, the peace I feel there. I also have a photo of one of my thin places as my wallpaper on my computer and another on my mobile phone to keep them near to me when I am far away from them.

It is not just the physical image I keep from these thin places, though. The powerful spiritual encounter stays, also. By bringing myself into the present moment, I re-encounter that experience afresh right here. I have my own particular techniques for dropping into this reality; other people have different ones but I'll share mine here. Firstly, I bring myself to a physical awareness of the present moment by pressing the tips of my thumbs and third fingers together. I breathe deeply in and out, then I visualise a white protective mist around me. When this is done, it's time for the 'beam me up Scotty' experience of detaching from the present environment and placing myself, through visualisation, on the beach or at the lakeside. If necessary, I can still be looking at, smiling, nodding, listening to the people around me but my spirit is also somewhere else, as well as here, getting me the energy, strength and wisdom I need and protecting me from negative influences.

Our development as spiritual beings is firstly for our own well-being and self-expression but that is not the only end; in fact it is a beginning which leads us on to other ends. When we are free from the plague of self-doubt and self-obsession; when we are comfortable with ourselves and have learnt to protect ourselves appropriately, when our spirits are free to guide us, then we can begin the task of healing each other and our world.

The Celts saw no division between sacred and secular; they would have been puzzled by the modern propensity for describing some things as profane and others as sacred. It is when we see all things are holding the divine within them that we can begin to understand the true nature and purpose of life. Those who curse the bluebottle but praise the bumble bee would do well to remember that onions are pollinated by bluebottles!

It is in this context of a sacred world, sacred in both its light and dark areas, its pain and its pleasure, that we can understand a spirituality of love. Our ministry to each other is one that accepts the glory and the shame and treats them with the same humility. It is one which looks on the best and worst a person can offer and offers both aspects the same healing love. A love which accepts and respects humanity as it is and not as we wish it were. A humanity that is instructed by the spirit, the Divine within us, reaching out to the Divine within the other.

This spirituality involves risk; the risk of making ourselves vulnerable to one another. It is not the cosy, warm feeling, where we are safe in a huddle of similar thinking people, that some are tempted to turn Christianity into. This is the open, challenging love that stretches us and makes us into the people we truly are. It is a lifelong adventure, an ongoing education that hones and sharpens our spiritual, emotional, mental and physical skills. It is swimming against the current of the modern world but if the waves occasionally throw us about, rush over our heads and momentarily plunge us beneath the waters, we will certainly know we are alive and in that moment of challenge, we will know the presence of the Divine holding us.

Hawks
Still-winged they glide
Trusting themselves
To the invisible force
Holding them aloft
As they ride its currents.
I feel the exhilaration
Of their air-surfing;
Risking, trusting, knowing
There will be no fatal free fall.
In the midst of this sorrow
You have borne me on your breath
And have not let me fall.
14.5.08

This spirituality of love involves being grown up and accepting the responsibility to walk away from unhealthy situations and relationships. It leads to speaking our truth, rather than pussy-footing around issues for fear of losing popularity. It means standing up for the voiceless, the oppressed, the marginalised and not being afraid to be publicly associated with them. It means passionately engaging with our planet and the other species who are unfortunate in having to share it with the human race. Most challenging of all, it means accepting the love poured out for us from a passionate and intimate Divinity who requires us to love and accept ourselves.

The first time I asked whether other people had those critical thoughts in their heads, I knew I was taking a risk but I am so glad that I did! It gave me permission to begin this amazing journey of mind, emotion, body and spirit and to begin to accept that God really is Love and I am a child of God, just as you are a child of God.

This is a journey we can begin, and begin again, at any and every moment because it is a journey of the present moment; the journey of eternity as it presents itself to us right now.

May you find peace in moments
That spill out into your life;
Love that heals your wounds,
Friends for the journey
And a Quiet Mind

The Woman with the Perfume

Many years ago, a woman created a beautiful perfume. It was rich and pure and utterly exquisite. It quickly became immensely popular and soon, as it became more and more sought after, it came to be known as the costliest perfume in the world.

A certain, wealthy woman was given several bottles of this perfume by her husband, over a number of years. She seldom wore the scent, however, because she was completely lacking in self-esteem and the perfume simply exacerbated this feeling. She locked the bottles in a dark cupboard where, she told herself, it would be safe because it would neither lose its scent nor be stolen. She resolved to forget about the legacy of the costliest perfume in the world. However, its presence in that cupboard haunted her; it was a constant, invisible reminder that she was simply not good enough for something of such beauty and value! As she grew older, her self-esteem diminished further and the more she knew she was 'not good enough', the worse she felt and the worse she felt, the more she allowed people to treat her badly. Her life seemed to plunge downwards on a spiral in which she allowed herself to be mistreated and abused until she finally despised herself so badly, that she had lost the will to go on.

One summer afternoon, as she was walking through the town, feeling utterly wretched, with a dark hopelessness enveloping her, she contemplated how she would either have to die or change her life completely. Walking with her head down, she stumbled into a sign outside the Town Hall. Stepping back, she read the words. 'Amazing Life Coach and Teacher in Town. One day only!' It seemed like an answer to a prayer she hadn't quite uttered! She found herself entering the building on autopilot and slinking into a seat at the back of the room. She listened intently as a man at the front of the room spoke about life as a gift; about how valuable each person was to God; about making your own choices and choosing life in all its fullness. He had a wonderful smile, penetrating eyes an intoxicating voice. He laughed frequently as he spoke and he talked about things that she recognised in her life. Other people were nodding understanding and for the first time in her life, she no longer felt alone. She understood what he was saying and saw for herself how she had allowed people to walk over her. She realised that she was valuable, loveable and good enough! She knew she had the power to change her own life.

At the end of the meeting, she left the building in a flush of euphoria and raced home. She wanted to say thank you to the teacher and she knew just how she would do it! On reaching her home, she ran upstairs and opened the cupboard where the perfume was hidden; she took out one of the bottles of perfume and began the journey back to town with it.

Inside the building again, she saw that it was now set out for a formal dinner and the teacher was the guest of honour on the top table. She felt afraid and tempted to leave; perhaps she was being sentimental and silly. Then she remembered the difference his words had made and her sense of gratitude gave her the courage to make her way up to that top table and right beside his seat. She looked down; he was wearing sandals on otherwise bare feet; she crouched down beside his chair. As she did so, her emotions overwhelmed her; all those feelings she'd kept locked inside her for so many years welled up, poured out of her eyes and down her cheeks. Her tears dropped onto his feet. She panicked; she had no towel to wipe his feet dry; then she thought about her long hair and quickly wiped the tears away with it. She opened the bottle of perfume and did what she had come to do; she poured the beautiful scent over his feet and with it her eternal gratitude. She heard him say something and she looked up and in his eyes saw such love and acceptance, her heart wanted to burst!

The man who had organised the dinner came over to the table and looked at her down his nose with its flared nostrils and through his tight lipped, disapproving mouth said to the teacher, "If you knew what kind of woman she is!" adding a snort of disgust to push the message home.

Her heart missed a beat and she felt her fragile, newfound self-esteem begin to crumble. She was on her way back to that familiar place of shame and doubt when she heard the teacher say to the man, "You're a fine one to talk, Simon!" She heard some of the other guests chuckle and mutter approvingly and then the teacher turned back to her and smiled. He said, "Thank you so much for your love and care! Now you go and live your life, love yourself and be free!"

.

References

Chapters 3 & 4
'The Summons', words by John L. Bell and Graham Maule, copyright © 1987 WGRG Iona Community, Glasgow G2 3DH, Scotland. Reproduced by permission. www.wgrg.co.uk

Chapter 5
Quote from pages 69-70 of 'Anam Cara' by John O'Donahue, copyright © 1997 by John O'Donahue. Originally published in Great Britain by Bantam Press, a division of Transworld Publishers, 61-63 Uxbridge Road, London W5 5SA. A division of the Random House Group Ltd.

The Prayer of Access. CIW publications, 39 Cathedral Road, Cardiff CF11 9FX. Reproduced with permission, the Church In Wales.

'Touching Place', words by John L. Bell and Graham Maule, copyright © 1987 WGRG Iona Community, Glasgow G2 3DH, Scotland. Reproduced by permission. www.wgrg.co.uk

Chapter 10
The Collect for the Twenty-first Sunday after Trinity is taken from The Book of Common Prayer. Published by The Syndics of Cambridge University Press, Bentley House, 200 Euston Road, London NW1 2DB.

B O O K S

O is a symbol of the world, of oneness and unity. In different cultures it also means the "eye," symbolizing knowledge and insight. We aim to publish books that are accessible, constructive and that challenge accepted opinion, both that of academia and the "moral majority."

Our books are available in all good English language bookstores worldwide. If you don't see the book on the shelves ask the bookstore to order it for you, quoting the ISBN number and title. Alternatively you can order online (all major online retail sites carry our titles) or contact the distributor in the relevant country, listed on the copyright page.

See our website **www.o-books.net** for a full list of over 500 titles, growing by 100 a year.

And tune in to myspiritradio.com for our book review radio show, hosted by June-Elleni Laine, where you can listen to the authors discussing their books.